Abai

Book of Songs

Abai
Book of Songs

Rendered by John Burnside

Signal

Signal Books
Oxford

First published in 2020 by the Embassy of Kazakhstan
in the United Kingdom via
Signal Books
West Wing Studios
Unit 166, The Mall
Luton, LU1 2TL
www.signalbooks.co.uk

A catalogue record for this book is available from the British Library.

ISBN 978-1-909930-93-3 (paper)

Cover Design: Tora Kelly
Typesetting: Tora Kelly
Front Cover Image: 'Taņšolpan' by Malik Mukanov
Signal Books is an imprint of Arthur H. Stockwell Limited

CONTENTS

Abai's Songs *by John Burnside* 2
Music in Translation *by Simon Wills* 5
Octaves 8
I Have Grown Weary 14
What Do You Want from Me? 16
Blessings on You 18
The Child Who Is Loved 20
My Soul, You Are Charmed by Nothing 22
The Apple of My Eye 24
Hypocrite 26
The Earth Turns Slow in Autumn 28
The Moon 30
You Could Not Love Me, nor I, You 32
If One Outweighs Another 33
The Mood Is Strong 36
Remembering Youth 38
If I Should Die 40
Fine Outside, I'm Dead Within 42
The Grey Mist Turns 43
A Tree Fell 46
I Had to Reveal All My Love 49
You Were Sent to Me by God 52
From the Terek River 56
In The Still of Night 58
Žoķtau 60
Toržorģa 63
May Night 64
Želdìrme 66
Notes 67

Abai. Books of Songs

To commemorate the 175th anniversary of the great Kazakh poet, philosopher, and enlightener Abai Ķūnanbajūly, for the first time in history, the Embassy of the Republic of Kazakhstan in the United Kingdom of Great Britain and Northern Ireland initiated and published the collection of Abai's songs in English – *Abai. Book of Songs*.

The brightest representative of the 19th century Kazakh intellectual world, Abai is widely considered the founding father of the modern Kazakh written literature, a cultural reformer, and a vital bridge between Kazakh and European cultures.

Along with Abai's literary work, the Kazakh culture inherited his rich and complex musical legacy, which has become an inherent part of a Kazakh cultural identity. Abai's songs are dear to our hearts as we grew up on them.

This edition includes three musical compositions (*kùj*) and twenty-three songs attributed to Abai, as well as scores and lyrics available in English for the first time. The book also refers the reader via QR codes to performed Kazakh versions of Abai's works.

The National Bureau of Translations of Kazakhstan, Zifa Auezova, Rose Kudabayeva, Aknur Toleubayeva and Assiya Issemberdiyeva provided the bridge translations of the poems, while the celebrated Scottish poet, Professor John Burnside, offered versions of Abai's lyrics that not only render the meaning, but also capture the original Kazakh metre as close as possible. Professor Simon Wills of the Guildhall School of Music and Drama was kind enough to contribute to this volume with his insightful foreword on the spirit of Kazakh music.

This book would not be complete without the support of the Kazakh National University of Arts headed by a renowned Kazakh virtuoso violinist Aiman Mussakhajayeva, as well as prominent Kazakh folk singers and musicians, Yerlan Ryskali, Perizat Turarova, Ayaulym Kamazhan, Askar Mukiyat, and Rustem Nurkenov who granted our readers the opportunity to enjoy the beauty of Abai's songs and *kùjs* through their performances.

Some of the recorded performances are part of the *Қазақтың Дәстүрлі 1000 Әні (1000 Traditional Kazakh Songs)* collection, included in this book with the permission of the El Production Centre.

All of the recordings of Abai's works included in this volume are available at www.kitap.kz, whom we thank for providing their platform.

And finally, we thank the project's coordinators, Zhanbolat Ussenov and Aigerim Seisembayeva of the Embassy of Kazakhstan in the UK, as well as Assiya Issemberdiyeva of the National Bureau of Translations of Kazakhstan, who carefully handled every step of the production process.

We sincerely hope our readers enjoy this unique book which puts the spotlight on an important part of Kazakh culture and history and trust that it sparks a passion for an in-depth exploration of Kazakh musical tradition.

Erlan Idrissov
Ambassador of Kazakhstan to the United Kingdom

ABAI'S SONGS

John Burnside

When approaching an unfamiliar poet, especially one from a culture or time period very different from one's own, it is tempting to look for parallels with more familiar voices, at least as a starting point. Caution is always advised when taking this approach, but the tactic can be useful in finding paths into the work of a writer whose allusions, philosophical or religious reference points and, most importantly, formal techniques, present a challenge. So it is that, in Abai's case, in spite of some obvious cultural stumbling blocks for a non-Kazakh reader, a wide range of lyrical kindred spirits comes to mind. Historically, for example, we might find common ground with a poet like Jonathan Swift, who similarly combined satiric wit and keen social observation with tender and intimate poetry of love and friendship; while, coming from an entirely different angle, the finest of the Delta Blues masters (a musician-poet like Charlie Patton, say) may spring to mind as a similarly adept practitioner of the oral tradition. As a Scottish writer, however, the figure I turned to most frequently as I approached the task of versioning Abai was Robert Burns. We find common ground with Burns even in Abai's prose, but those shared perspectives become even more evident when we compare the poems and songs directly. Like Burns, Abai is a poet who knows the tribulations of romantic love; like Burns he has a keen eye for hypocrisy, societal flaws and political corruption; like Burns he loves the land. It is clear, also, that both poets draw a good deal of their power, Antaeus-like, from the home-ground of an oral tradition in which tradition is invoked and honoured even as it is imaginatively renewed.

Just one example might illustrate their kinship on the moral and political front. In 1791, Burns wrote the poem 'Such a Parcel of Rogues in a Nation', a fierce condemnation of those Company of Scotland investors who, having lost their money in an ill-advised colonial adventure in Panama, agreed to sign over the historically independent Scottish parliament to English control (in 1707's so-called 'Act of Union'), for which betrayal their losses were reimbursed in full, (some even received a bonus for their work):

Fareweel to a' our Scottish fame,
Fareweel our ancient glory,
Fareweel ev'n to the Scottish name,
Sae fam'd in martial story.
Now Sark rins o'er the Solway sands,
And Tweed rins to the ocean,
To mark where England's province stands -
Such a parcel of rogues in a nation.

What force or guile could not subdue,
Thro' many warlike ages,

Is wrought now by a coward few
For hireling traitor's wages.
The English steel we could disdain;
Secure in valour's station;
But English gold has been our bane —
Such a parcel of rogues in a nation.

Leaving aside some disingenuous references to a romanticised Scottish past, this song-poem works, not only as an indictment of a very specific parcel of rogues, but also as a bitter satire for the ages – and it has been spoken and sung since in many different contexts (a good example is the famous Dubliners' recording, where this Irish Republican group emphasises the role of 'English gold' in Irish history). It is by no means a stretch to see how Burns' tone, his method and his unsparing wit parallel Abai's equally sharp critiques of his own countrymen when, like the villain of the song 'The Hypocrite', they descend to similar levels of betrayal and self-abasement:

Lies are his trade,
Friends are betrayed,
He welches on every deal.
He finds his man
And takes what he can,
Till nothing is left to steal.

Turn the page, however, and in both cases we find unique examples of lyric tenderness, whether for the land, or for a beloved friend. In such works, the power of an apparent simplicity, founded in a strong oral tradition, gives each poet a power for the ages, a true universality that is impossible to falsify.

Another, more modern, parallel with Abai's lyric impulse can be found in the work of Bob Dylan, especially the Dylan of the Christian period, where the songs use Biblical references to attack many of the same political and societal sins with which Abai engages as a Muslim. Here the similarities are even more useful to consider in one respect at least; for where Burns stands outside the religious orthodoxy of his day, mocking not just ordinary hypocritical churchgoers (or 'unco guid' as he so perfectly describes this very Scottish specimen) he also attacks the institution itself from what seems to be an agnostic position. By contrast, Abai and Dylan invoke those nominally orthodox values that are being flagrantly disregarded by their self-serving neighbours. For Abai and Dylan, the position taken is that of the true believer, who stands by a moral and spiritual code that should – but does not – inform their immediate community. Just as Abai invokes Islamic values to reinforce his critiques, so Dylan calls upon both Old and New Testament imagery, language and teachings in his work from the late 1970s onward, (that is, beginning with the *Slow Train Coming* album of 1979, for which he cites as an overall guiding principle the verse from Matthew's Gospel (7:12): "Therefore all things whatsoever ye would that men should do to you: do ye even so to them: for this is the law and the prophets"). It is worth noting that, especially in the work he did on *Infidels* (including the powerful 'Foot of Pride' which was recorded during the album sessions, but not released till later) Dylan brings together a New Testament emphasis on love with an Old Testament consideration of judgment to show that, as much as love must guide our dealings with others, we cannot dispense with judgment – and, in fact, love that foregoes judgment is not love at all, but some form of indifference, indulgence or moral laziness. I think that, had they met, Abai and Dylan would wholeheartedly have agreed on this.

Yet, even as we draw these parallels to get a handle on a writer whose references – both cultural and religious – may sometimes puzzle us, as non-Kazakh readers, what very soon comes across is the strong sense of universality, grounded in oral tradition, that Abai's work shares with that of poets like Burns, Bob Dylan and Charlie Patton. In the final analysis, it is his humanity that commends Abai to us; his tenderness, his fierce judgments, his love of the land and his sometimes frustrated sense of community all speak to us, as they would speak to readers and listeners anywhere, no matter what their traditions and cultural referents might be. All too often, Abai's pessimism is highlighted – and it is true that, like Burns, like Dylan, he perceives and feels keenly the sins of his fellow men and the harm done to a land he loves – but this is to forget an insistent underlying thread of compassion, even of hope, in all these poets' works, no matter how accurately they document the hard facts of communal existence. Along with Abai, we are moved to anger and sadness by the failings of humankind but, at the last, we also remember our own humanity, and with him, we are minded to think mercifully. Or, as Abai himself put it: "Let me leave you a written memento about the nature of humankind. Read it attentively and commit it lovingly to memory, for love alone is just reward for love."

MUSIC IN TRANSLATION

Simon Wills

Ibrahim Ķùnanbajùly (1845–1904), known all his life as Abai, grew up surrounded by music. Women sang for weddings, funerals and the fasting at Ramadan, they devised impromptu songs about their dinner guests or sang riddles to entertain them. Men and women engaged in poetical and musical duels called *ajtys*. These still exist today, and can take many forms; sometimes they set ever more challenging riddles to the contestants, they can be expressions of local pride, in which praise is extemporised for one tribe at the expense of another; and sometimes, naturally enough, young men and women compete in singing and joking about each other. Young Abai heard *kùj*, long narrative tone poems played on a *dombyra*, the strummed lute that is ever-present in Central Asian music. He was a skilful *dombyra* player himself, and created *kùjs* of his own: he called them 'stories without words.' Around the time he was born, a new type of lyrical song started to be sung, one characterised by a soaring opening cry, virtuoso wordless refrains and a marvellous irregularity in its verses that strained against the rhythmic boundaries of the melody. At school in Semej, Abai heard Russian music; works by Glinka, Anton Rubinstein and the sentimental songs that were then in vogue. In those days there were Tartar fugitives hiding in that part of the country. They brought their own music with them and added violins, mandolins, even accordions to the traditional instruments that were heard on the steppe.

It is no surprise that an unusual musician grew in such rich soil. Abai said 'I do not write my poems to amuse' and for him music, too, was more than entertainment. Delve into it with the eyes of thought, he said, and it will reveal life to you, as sharply seen as if it lay on the bed of a clean, clear stream. He called a song 'the shadow of a thought'; perhaps it was his sense of a tune's origin deep in the mind that drew him to the then unusual practice of assigning a melody to a specific poem, rather than letting it be a vehicle for any text whose metre happened to fit.

Descriptions of him agree that his voice was not strong or resonant, but it was by singing that Abai chose to share his work: he wrote down none of his melodies. A few were transcribed in the 1920s but most were notated in 1939, when the composer had been dead for thirty-five years. They were sung to the men who wrote them down by Abai's descendants. Memory, then, is the first of the translations through which his music has passed. In Kazakhstan, the power of recall was always prized: the loser of an *ajtys* was traditionally obliged afterwards to repeat the whole contest, from memory. Given such an ability to scan a musical horizon, descry its details and replicate them, we can speculate that what the transcribers heard was what Abai had sung, even across such a stretch of time; but we cannot know. It is equally possible that memory acted as a filter, preserving the strongest elements of a melody, or that the improvisatory nature of Kazakh singers led them to introduce variations and decorations.

In some ways it is surprising that Abai never learned musical notation. To write down a single line of melody is a simple skill, easily learned, but it is possible that he understood the limitations of western notation and chose not to engage with it. It is important to understand those limitations, for the writing down of his music is the second form of translation that we must consider. The thing we call 'normal' musical notation divides its octave into an evenly-spaced scale and rhythm is expressed as divisions of a more or less stable pulse. When this system tries to express complex rhythms, it locks them in narrow mathematical cages. It has no capacity at all for the inflections, microtones and colours that are part of the business of making music. John Burnside sometimes compares Abai to Bob Dylan: anyone who has purchased the sheet music to one of Dylan's songs or any other piece of popular music will be familiar with the slight sense of letdown that is felt when you get it home and realise that though some elements – the chords and a version of the tune – may be found on the page, most of the detail that makes the song truly itself is not there – because the notation is unequal to the task. In the second half of the twentieth century, new ways of writing music down were devised that were able to record more detail, but these were not available to Abai's transcribers. Reading what they wrote, it is easy to imagine them labouring to be faithful to the original with tools that were not really up to the job. They experimented with different divisions of the beat or with shifting metres and came as close as they could. What they produced is good music because the character and muscularity of the melody is there: in Abai's words 'it leaps, it soars; like a stream it flows along so quick and true.' Even so, anyone who has heard the scuttling of a *dombyra* or the decorations that so elaborately dress a Kazakh song well sung will understand that confining so subtle an art on so blunt a notation necessarily entails making another translation.

Then there is language. We often imagine a division between the melody and the words of a song, but the distinction is an artificial one; the music of the language is part of the music of the melody. When an Italian opera is put into English, a little of its lightness is lost: the tongue-and-teeth swagger of the original is gone but the English cannot flow because it is strapped to musical rhythms that were never intended for it. Many of the sounds that make Ķazaķ tili such a beautiful spoken language do not exist in English, which lacks crisp uvular consonants and the slow 'L' sound, made with the back of the tongue lifted, that are part of the word 'Ķūnanbajūly'; and English rarely assumes the regular surges that emanate from Ķazaķ tili's uniform stress on the last syllable of a word. The poems printed here in English have a wonderful rhythmic variety of their own; they balance vowels and consonants in a way that makes them eminently singable, but their topography is not the same as that of the melodies. To try to fit the one exactly onto the other would be to do violence to both.

With so many layers of translation between us and Abai, how can an English speaker hope to sing these songs? Kazakh musicians themselves provide the answer. If you search for Abai on the Internet, you will find many versions of his works; a single voice accompanied by a *dombyra*, operatic arrangements after the manner of Puccini, some that aspire to the style of Andrew Lloyd Webber and even rock versions sung on television talent shows. Abai's alloy of a style grew out of many elements, and his 'shadows of a thought' remain potent whatever ground they are cast onto. If you listen with the transcriptions of his music in your hand, you will notice that the modern arrangements tend to stick quite closely to the printed melody but the traditional renderings, those closest to Abai's own origins, do not. They take a song's shape, a memorable pattern of notes or any other part of the melody that catches the ear, and use them as the starting point for something new and alive. Sometimes the difference is a note or two, sometimes it amounts to an entirely new song. We should do the same. In any music, and certainly in this music, an authentic performance cannot be created by naming of parts. This is particularly so here, where there are so many parts which in our case we have not got. These musical and literary translations provide us with a route into an authentic performance, in the sense of using these words and music as seed of something true to the spirit of what Abai was.

The sky in Kazakhstan feels bigger than it does in Europe. You can look out of a train window and marvel at how little the landscape changes for mile after mile, hour after hour. In the south of the country they will take you up into the mountains so that you can breathe the cold air and perhaps see a bit of life as if on the bed of a clean, clear stream. A Kazakh singer opens him or herself to the sky and that immense steppe:

> ...the heart brims, the body rings
> All that is good in this world sings in a rhyme.

They do what comes naturally to them, and it is glorious. Perhaps it is not a very British thing to do, but if you want to sing these poems truthfully, absorb some things in this collection of melodies that please you – then throw back your head and sing.

OCTAVES
VERSION I

OCTAVES
VERSION II

OCTAVES
VERSION III

OCTAVES
VERSION IV

OCTAVES
VERSION V

OCTAVES
VERSION VI

OCTAVES

VERSION VII

OCTAVES
VERSION VIII

Octaves

From afar, it strikes,
Through your heart, it breaks,
Your body is racked with fever.
From Khiva, come quick,
So much is at stake,
Hunt down the wildest of creatures –
You can tell the truth, if you're strong,
With a silver tongue and a song.

No needle and thread,
Nor the bright steel blade
Can equal your skill in arts and crafts.
To the wise, a pearl,
A trifle, to fools,
They lack true wisdom, blind to your gifts.
Yet let not my voice speak in vain:
Truth cannot prevail with thoughtless men.

Bridge translation by Zifa Auezova

Segìz Aâķ

Alystan sermep
Žùrekten terbep
Šymyrlap bojġa žajylġan;
Ķiuadan šauyp
Ķisynyn tauyp
Taġyny žetìp ķajyrġan —
Tolġauy toķsan ķyzyl tìl,
Sôjlejmìn deseņ ôzìņ bìl.

Ôtkìrdìņ žùzì
Kestenìņ bìzì
Ôrnegìn sendej sala almas.
Bìlgenge maržan
Bìlmeske arzan
Nadandar bắhra ala almas.
Ķinalma beker tìl men žaķ,
Kôņìlsìz ķùlaķ ojġa olaķ.

Performed
by Zhusipbek
Yelebekov

Performed
by Yerlan
Ryskali

I HAVE GROWN WEARY

VERSION I

I HAVE GROWN WEARY

VERSION II

I HAVE GROWN WEARY

VERSION III

I HAVE GROWN WEARY

VERSION IV

I Have Grown Weary

I have grown weary
With pining for you each day.
My spirit is frayed.
These torments are planned, they say:
God proposes – and man?
How can he change God's plan?

May my voice sing on.
I have sickened from this pain.
My body grows numb
Since my sweetheart let me down.
My spirit swells with grief.
How can I find relief?

I miss you so much.
You never write any more.
I long for your touch.
I am wounded to the core.
This pain is so hard to hold,
My very bones turn cold.

If only this prayer
Would reach my love, I might dare
To summon a cure
To drive away all my cares.
When spirit cures its ills
Tormented flesh will heal.

Bridge translation by Zifa Auezova

Ķor Boldy Žanym

Ķor boldy žanym,
Sensìzde menìņ kùnìm,
Bek bìttì halìm,
Tağdyrdan kelgen zùlym.
Tağdyr etse Alla,
Ne kôrmejdì pắnde?

Sajraj ber tìlìm,
Sarġajġan soņ bùl dertten.
Bùgìldì belìm,
Žar tajġan soņ ắr sertten.
Ķamyryķty kôņìl,
Ķajtse bolar žeņìl?

Sağyndym senì,
Kôrmedìm dep kôp zaman.
Adam dep menì,
Salmadyņ sen hat mağan.
Žaj taba almaj žùrek,
Žasyġan soņ sùjek.

Bùl ķylġan zarym
Barsa žardyņ maņyna,
Ol – ķylġan dắrìm
Ġašyġymnyņ žanyna.
Oņaldyryp ojdy,
Tùzetpej me bojdy?

Performed by
Yerlan Ryskali

WHAT DO YOU WANT FROM ME?

VERSION I

What Do You Want from Me?

What is it you want from me?
You turn your back,
Your mood turns black.
You are false.
I can't keep track,
You mock –
Then you turn round and leave me be.

What do you want me to do?
You stay away,
Your fiancé
Is troubled.
Yet no-one says
You stray.
You torment me my whole life through.

My spirit soon will break.
My flesh is fire,
My heart, a pyre.
I'm burning.
I'm like a cur,
Whining.
You might as well have wrung my neck.

My love burns ever bright!
In times of woe,
When I'm near you
I despair
And say nothing.
Struck dumb!
My strength gives out, my mind's not right.

Bridge translation by Zifa Auezova

WHAT DO YOU WANT FROM ME?

VERSION II

Sen Menì Ne Etesìņ?

Sen menì ne etesìņ?
Menì tastap
Ôner bastap
Žajyņa
Žắne aldap
Arbap
Ôz betìņmen sen ketesìņ.

Nege ắure etesìņ?
Ķosylyspaj
Basylyspaj
Bajyņa
Žắne žattan
Baj tap
Ômìr bojy ķor etesìņ.

Et žùrek ôrtendì,
Ot bop žanyp,
Žalyn šalyp
Ìšìme
Ittej ķormyn
Zarmyn
Sen ùzdìņ ġoj bùl želkemdì.

Šyn ġašyķ men saġan!
Kejìp žùrsem
Senì kôrsem
Lắm-mim dep
Bìr sôz ajtar
Hal žoķ
Erìp keter boj sol zaman.

Performed by Perizat Turarova

BLESSINGS ON YOU
VERSION I

BLESSINGS ON YOU
VERSION II

BLESSINGS ON YOU

VERSION III

Blessings on You

Blessings on you, wondrous one,
Let me give you all I own.
Whenever I shall think of you
The tracks of my tears will burn.

Your like will not come again,
Not now, nor world without end.
To no one else can I speak
Of my passion, dearest friend.

A true heart gives all it can,
Its resolve will not be changed.
Whether or not I see you,
In my heart's heart, you will remain.

Bridge translation by Zifa Auezova

Ajttym Sa̋lem Ḳalam Ḳas

Ajttym sa̋lem ḳalam ḳas,
Saġan ḳúrban mal men bas.
Saġynġannan senì ojlap,
Keler kôzge ystyḳ žas.

Senen artyḳ žan tumas,
Tusa tuar artylmas.
Bìr ôzìṇnen basḳaġa
Yntyḳtyġym ajtylmas.

Asyl adam ajnymas,
Bìr betìnen ḳajyrylmas.
Kôrmesem de kôrsem de,
Kôṇìlìm senen ajyrylmas.

Performed
by Zhanibek
Karmenov

THE CHILD WHO IS LOVED

The Child Who Is Loved

The child who is loved, the happy child,
Brings light to the house, like the sun,
His parents are blessed, their hopes fulfilled,
Joy is theirs, and great renown.
But now he is grown,
Can he stand
With the men?

For him, they find the wisest teacher,
A living Sage, a master.
No one could have taught him better;
Still, he cannot find an answer.
Now, nothing matters,
All is chatter;
Hopes are shattered.

For when the spark fails to ignite,
When the spirit fails to sing,
When no great talent comes to light,
When ignorance clips his wings,
No future for him,
His soul grows dim.
Take warning!

Bridge translation by Zifa Auezova

Ata-Anaġa Kôz Ķuanyš

Ata-anaġa kôz ķuanyš –
Aldyna alġan erkesì.
Kôkìregìne kôp žùbanyš,
Gùldenìp oj ôlkesì.
Erkelìk kettì
Er žettì
Ne bìttì?

Oķytarsyņ moldaġa ony,
Ùjretersìņ ắr nenì.
Medeu etìp ojy sony,
Žany tynyštyķ kôrmedì.
Žasynda kùttì
Dắme ettì
Bosķa ôttì.

Ata kôņìl žanbasa bìr,
Artyķ ôner šyķpasa.
El tanymaj ùj tanyp ķùr,
Šaruasyn da ùķpasa –
Ùmìtì ķajda?
Sony ojla
Abajla!

Performed
by Zhusipbek
Yelebekov

MY SOUL, YOU ARE CHARMED BY NOTHING

VERSION I

MY SOUL, YOU ARE CHARMED BY NOTHING

VERSION II

My Soul, You Are Charmed by Nothing

My soul, you are charmed by nothing,
But you never quit your singing.
When a thought comes good in a song
My sorrows are gone. I'm smiling!

May my grief pour forth in a song,
May my blackest thoughts come calling,
Redden my eyes with weeping.
Let bitter tears come streaming.

What can a fool comprehend?
Can ideas take root in such a mind?
May he who is wise, with the light
Of fire in his heart, understand.

Let song rise high, like a spark,
Lighting a path through the dark,
When it burns out, spent and cold,
May its wise words find their mark.

Bridge translation by Zifa Auezova

Ôzgege, Kôṇìlìm, Toârsyṇ

Ôzgege, kôṇìlìm, toârsyṇ,
Ôleṇdì ķajtìp ķoârsyṇ?
Ony ajtķanda tolġanyp,
Ìštegì derttì žoârsyṇ.

Sajra da zarla ķyzyl tìl,
Ķara kôṇìlìm oânsyn.
Žylasyn, kôzden žas aķsyn,
Omyrauym boâlsyn.

Ķara basķan, ķaṇġyġan,
Has nadan nenì ùġa alsyn?
Kôkìregìnde oty bar,
Ķùlaġyn ojly er salsyn.

Ấuelesìn ķalķysyn,
Ot-žalyn bop šalķysyn.
Žylaj-žyrlaj ôlgende,
Arttaġyġa sôz ķalsyn.

Performed by Yerlan Ryskali

THE APPLE OF MY EYE

VERSION I

THE APPLE OF MY EYE

VERSION II

THE APPLE OF MY EYE

VERSION III

THE APPLE OF MY EYE

VERSION IV

The Apple of My Eye	Kôzìmnìṇ Ķarasy
My midnight and my noon, She is the sun, and the moon, The apple of my eye, Nothing can heal this wound.	Kôzìmnìṇ ķarasy, Kôṇìlìmnìṇ sanasy, Bìtpejdì ìšìmde, Ġašyķtyṇ žarasy.
The wisest amongst men, The best and the brightest minds, No matter how they try, Her equal can't be found.	Ķazaķtyṇ danasy, Žasy ùlken aġasy. Bar demes sendej bìr Adamnyṇ balasy.
I weep from joy and pain, These hot tears scald and sting, I know what I must say When we two meet again:	Žylajyn žyrlajyn, Aġyzyp kôz majyn. Ajtuġa kelgende, Ķalķama sôz dajyn.
I will be true and plain, Courteous, calm and kind, Nothing can bar my way: Surely she knows my mind!	Žùrekten ķozġajyn, Ấdepten ozbajyn. Ôzì de bìlmej me, Kôp sôjlep sozbajyn.

Bridge translation by Zifa Auezova

Performed by Madeniet Yeshekeyev

HYPOCRITE
VERSION I

Hypocrite

If I should meet
The hypocrite
Who twists his words into knots,
I hide my face
From that disgrace
And take my leave like a shot!

He, he would say,
In every way
Is flawless – pure as snow.
At large, he's warm,
Skinflint at home,
He breaks his vows just for show.

He'll wish you luck,
Then grab your stock.
Give nothing, he'll soon be gone.
He sets his trap
And never gives up,
Till he's captured a rich man.

Lies are his trade,
Friends are betrayed,
He welches on every deal.
He finds his man
And takes what he can,
Till nothing is left to steal.

Bridge translation by Zifa Auezova

HYPOCRITE

VERSION II

HYPOCRITE

VERSION III

Bojy Bùlġaņ

Bojy bùlġaņ
Sôzì žylmaņ
Kìmdì kôrsem men sonan
Bettì bastym
Ķatty sastym
Tùra ķaštym žalma-žan.

Ôz ojynda
Tùl bojynda
Bìr mìnì žoķ pendesìp,
Tùzde myrzaņ
Ùjde syrdaņ
Sôzì ķylžaņ erkesìp.

Bas ķùrasyp
Mal sùrasyp
Bermegenmen ketìser.
Adam aulap
Sypyra saulap
Bajdy žaulap žetìser.

Sôz ķydyrtķan
Žùrt ķùtyrtķan
Antyn, aryn saudalap.
Bùtty-šatty
Ùj sanatty
Bajdan atty almalap.

Performed
by Zhanibek
Karmenov

THE EARTH TURNS SLOW IN AUTUMN

VERSION I

THE EARTH TURNS SLOW IN AUTUMN

VERSION II

The Earth Turns Slow in Autumn

The earth turns slow in autumn.
If it stopped what would winter say?
The whole village waits for the sun.
Will the grass grow tall, if we pray?

Can a tulip bloom in the cold?
Spring snow blankets the houses.
But kindle a fire in the hall –
Cold as it seems, it blazes.

Bridge translation by Zifa Auezova

Ķarašada Ômìr Tùr

Ķarašada ômìr tùr,
Toķtatsaṇ, toķsan kôner me?
Arttaġy majda kôṇìl žùr,
Žalynsaṇ, ķajtyp keler me?

Majdaġy žùrttyṇ ìšì – ķar,
Bắjšešek ķarġa ôner me?
Ìšìnde kìmnìṇ oty bar,
Ķar žausa da sôner me?

Performed
by Perizat
Turarova

THE MOON
VERSION I

The Moon

No wind tonight, just the moon
Flooding the lakeside with silver,
Over the valley, all alone,
Some low huts down by the river.

A spreading tree, noble and bright,
Rustles its leaves in the cool night.
Under the green hills, still in the light,
The earth is concealed from our sight.

The peaks ring out with echoes
Of barking dogs and voices.
Did you travel here to follow
The road to these far places?

You heart wavered, all alone,
Flushed with fever, cold as stone,
You could hardly breathe, strength all gone,
Fear touched you for no reason.

Did he not stand here, head bowed down,
Hiding his face in her breast?
Unable to speak, and no sound
But his pounding heart in his chest?

Bridge translation by Zifa Auezova

THE MOON
VERSION II

Želsìz Tùnde Žaryķ Aj

Želsìz tùnde žaryķ aj,
Sắulesì suda dìrìldep,
Auyldyņ žany tereņ saj,
Tasyġan ôzen gùrìldep.

Ķalyņ aġaš žapyraġy
Sybyrlasyp ôzdì-ôzì,
Kôrìnbej žerdìņ topyraġy,
Ķùlpyrġan žasyl žer žùzì.

Tau žaņġyryġyp ắn ķosyp
Ùrgen itpen ajtaķķa.
Kelmep pe edìņ žol tosyp
Žolyġuġa aulaķķa?

Tajmaņdamaj tamylžyp,
Bìr suynyp bìr ysyp,
Dem ala almaj damyl ķyp,
Eleņ ķaġyp bos šošyp.

Sôz ajta almaj bôgelìp,
Dùrsìl ķaġyp žùregì,
Türmap pa edì sùjenìp,
Tamaķķa kìrìp iegì?

Performed by
Adilet Musa

YOU COULD NOT LOVE ME, NOR I, YOU

You Could Not Love Me, nor I, You

You could not love me, nor I, you,
That was the heartbreak of my life.
To wed was more than we could do.
We can never be man and wife.

Bridge translation by Zifa Auezova

Sùjsìne Almadym, Sùjmedìm

Sùjsìne almadym sùjmedìm,
Sùjegìm žasyp sor ķalyņ.
Sùjìsìp saġan timedìm,
Bola almadym senìņ žaryņ.

Performed
by Perizat
Turarova

IF ONE OUTWEIGHS ANOTHER

VERSION I

IF ONE OUTWEIGHS ANOTHER

VERSION II

IF ONE OUTWEIGHS ANOTHER

VERSION III

If One Outweighs Another

If one outweighs another,
If wit were subject to measure,
The learned man would show his skill,
The fool would remain a bungler.

The wise man only gets wiser,
Unlike the dolt and the idler,
There's nothing you can teach a fool,
Non-one he knows is that clever.

Bridge translation by Zifa Auezova

Bìreuden Bìreu Artylsa

Bìreuden bìreu artylsa,
Ôner ôlšenìp tartylsa,
Oķyġan, bìlgen bìlgen-aķ,
Nadan nadan-aķ san ķylsa.

Oķyġan bìler ắr sôzdì,
Nadandaj bolmas aķ kôzdì.
Nadan žôndìge žôn kelmej,
Bìler ķajdaġy šắrgezdì.

Performed
by Yerlan
Ryskali

THE MOOD IS STRONG

The Mood Is Strong

From time to time, thoughts come clear, the mood is strong,
All the powers of the mind pour forth in song,
Upside down, and inside out, it twists the mind,
And in a rhyme, in tempo, the spirit sings.

It leaps; it soars; like a stream, it flows along
So quick and true, the heart brims, the body rings.
All that is good in this world sings in a rhyme.
The heedless mind could never rise to such a thing.

The heart is roused by a song, what it confides
Is the message, a plain truth that the music hides:
Joyful, at times, and though tears are never far,
The soul is soothed, like a child, and its pain subsides.

But a song can be foolish as well as wise,
Hard on the ears, discordant, an awful noise.
Contrariwise, a fine song, with real meaning,
Like a wise speech, it lifts you and brings you joy.

Life begins in loving warmth, the end is ice.
Happy the game, at the start, sad at the close.
But listen well, for this song has no ending,
Fresh from the source, like a spring, it wells and flows

Bridge translation by Zifa Auezova

Kôņìl Ķu̇sy Ķu̇jķylžyr Šartarapķa

Kôņìl ķu̇sy ķu̇jķylžyr šartarapķa,
Adam ojy tùrlenìp auġan šaķta.
Salġan a̋n kôleņkesì sol kôņìldìņ,
Taktysyna bilesìn ol ķu̇laķķa.

Šyrķap, ķalķyp, sorġalap tamylžidy,
Žùrek terbep oâtar basta midy.
Bu̇l dùnienìņ la̋zza̋tì ba̋rì sonda,
Ojsyz ķu̇laķ ala almas ondaj syjdy.

U̇jyķtap žatķan žùrektì a̋n oâtar,
Ùnnìņ ta̋ttì oralġan ma̋nì oâtar.
Kejì zauyķ kejì mu̇ņ dertìn ķozġap,
Žas balaša kôņìldì žaķsy uatar.

A̋nnìņ de estìsì bar, eserì bar,
Tyņdaušynyņ ķu̇laġyn keserì bar.
Aķyldynyņ sôzìndej ojly kùjdì
Tyņdaġanda kôņìldìņ ôserì bar.

Ômìrdìņ aldy – ystyķ, arty – suyķ,
Aldy – ojyn, art žaġy mu̇ņġa žuyķ.
Žaķsy a̋ndì tyņdasaņ oj kôzìņmen,
Ômìr sa̋ule kôrseter sudaj tùnyķ.

Performed
by Perizat
Turarova

REMEMBERING YOUTH

Remembering Youth

Do you sometimes think of your youth?
When each man you met was a friend.
Days without sorrow, free of strife –
Carefree and true to the end?

O, the years, the years, and the hours,
The wind and the sun and the showers,
Faded, they fell, like flowers,
And all the bright things that were ours.

You can't help but grieve, and complain
For those you once loved who are gone,
Gone, now, it's all in your mind,
Like the love that was once your own.

Bridge translation by Zifa Auezova

Esìṇde Bar Ma Žas Kùnìṇ

Esìṇde bar ma žas kùnìṇ,
Kôkìregìṇ tolyḳ basyṇ bos,
Ḳajġysyz, ojsyz mas kùnìṇ –
Kìmdì kôrseṇ bấrì dos.

Mahabbat, ḳyzyḳ mal men baḳ
Kôrìnušì edì dosḳa ortaḳ.
Ùmìt žaḳyn kôṇìl aḳ,
Bolar ma sondaj ḳyzyḳ šaḳ?

Ḳùdaj-au, ḳajda sol žyldar,
Mahabbat, ḳyzyḳ mol žyldar?
Aḳyryn, aḳyryn šegìnìp,
Alystap kettì-au ḳùrġyrlar!

Performed
by Perizat
Turarova

IF I SHOULD DIE

If I Should Die

If I should die, will I lie in cold black earth?
Will my tongue, so sharp in life, forego its wrath?
And my heart, where love and hate have always warred,
Will it not freeze in the paws of icy death?

And will Fate, that finds us all, not find me out?
To some it comes swift and hard, to others late.
And will my heart, unbroken, although it erred,
Be cruelly judged, though it lies deep in the grave?

Inside I am blood and bile, outside I'm stern,
Soon I will leave, since nothing is mine to win.
This telltale song betrays me to all the world,
so enough! I've said my piece, and now I'm done.

Bridge translation by Zifa Auezova

Ôlsem, Ornym Ķara Žer Syz Bolmaj Ma

Ôlsem, ornym ķara žer syz bolmaj ma?
Ôtkìr tìl bìr ủâlšaķ ķyz bolmaj ma?
Mahabbat ġadauatpen majdandasķan
Ķajran menìņ žùregìm mủz bolmaj ma?

Amalsyz taġdyr bìr kùn kez bolmaj ma?
Bìreuge žaj, bìreuge tez bolmaj ma?
Asau žùrek aâġyn šalys basķan
Žerìn tauyp artķyġa sôz bolmaj ma?

Ìšìm – tolġan u men ôrt syrtym dùrdej,
Men kelmeske ketermìn tùk ôndìrmej.
Ôleņ šìrkìn ôsekšì žùrtķa žaâr,
Syrymdy toķtatajyn ajta bermej.

Performed
by Yerlan
Ryskali

FINE OUTSIDE, I'M DEAD WITHIN

Fine Outside, I'm Dead Within

Fine outside, I'm dead within.
This day's comrade, best of men,
Will let me down, with the dawn.
Oh, God, what good can be done?
When I'm at home, I argue:
Like a torrent, on and on,
My anger pours forth; with strangers
I'm timid and put upon.

When you're tested, and you stand
In a storm of strife and spin,
No good comes to men like you
Try as you might, you don't win.
The contest is harsh, my friend,
But don't slam the door when it's done.
Though things may be fine for now,
One day you'll have to come in.

Bridge translation by Rose Kudabayeva

Ìšìm Ôlgen, Syrtym Sau

Ìšìm ôlgen syrtym sau,
Kôrìngenge dejmìn-au:
Bùgìngì dos erteņ žau,
Men ne ķyldym âpyrmau?!
Ôz ùjìnde ôzendej
Kùrkìrejdì ajtsa dau.
Kìsì aldynda kìrbeņdep,
Šaban, šardaķ žắne šau.

Top bolġanda kôrersìņ
Tùrlì daudy žùz tarau.
Aâġynda sendejler
Kôrmej žùr me ķantalau?
Ķajta kìrer esìktì
Ķatty serìppe žarķyn-au!
Žetìlseņ de, žetseņ de,
Kerek kùnì bìr bar-au.

Performed by Askar Mukiyat

THE GREY MIST TURNS
VERSION I

THE GREY MIST TURNS
VERSION II

THE GREY MIST TURNS
VERSION III

The Grey Mist Turns

The grey mist turns to drizzle,
The fine coat is streaked and stained.
The young man weeps and mingles
The salt of his tears with the rain.

You're not a child, stop crying.
Remember, God is watching.
Mend your ways.
Sing His praise.

They say that Adam was beguiled
By Eve, his wife's seduction
Holy Eden was defiled,
The penance for both, expulsion.

Women are fickle, so I'm told,
One day they're warm, next day cold.
Show some grace!
Wash your face!

Bridge translation by Assiya Issemberdiyeva

Súrġylt Túman Dym Bùrkìp

Súrġylt túman dym bùrkìp,
Barķyt bešpent sulajdy.
Žeņìmenen kôz sùrtìp,
Súrlanyp žìgìt žylajdy.

A̋jelmìsìņ, žylama,
Ta̋uekel ķyl Ķúdaġa!
Ôleņ ajt,
Ùjge ķajt!

Ataņdy anaņ azġyryp,
Túrġyzbaġan bejìške.
Allasy ony žazġyryp,
A̋keldì bastap kejìske.

A̋jelde ešbìr opa žoķ,
Bùgìn – žalyn, erteņ – šoķ.
Beldì bu,
Bettì žu!

Performed by Talgat Abugazy

A TREE FELL
VERSION I

A TREE FELL
VERSION II

A TREE FELL

VERSION III

A Tree Fell

A tree fell, I saw it drop, a tall birch tree,
It tumbled and crashed to earth, submissively,
A tree fell but no one heard the plaintive cry
That rang out, and no one saw, as they rode by.

A deer fell, I saw it die, a playful deer,
It was shot and left wounded, gasping for air.
It was crushed, it was bleeding, its heart giving out.
To see how it suffered was too much to bear.

My old love was inconstant, one I held dear,
I lost faith in life's sweetness, burdened with care,
It cut to the heart of me; now, beyond hope,
I go on, but the memory always stands near.

Bridge translation by Assiya Issemberdiyeva

Men Kôrdìm Ủzyn Ḳajyṇ Ḳủlaġanyn

Men kôrdìm ủzyn ḳajyṇ ḳủlaġanyn,
Bas ủryp ḳara žerge sủlaġanyn.
Žapyraġy sarġajyp, ôlìmsìrep,
Bajġủstyṇ kìm tyṇdajdy žylaġanyn?

Men kôrdìm ojnap žủrgen ḳyzyl kììk,
Keudesìne myltyḳtyṇ oġy tììp,
Ḳalžyrap, ḳansyraġan, ḳabaḳ tủsken,
Kìmge batar ol bajġủs tartḳan kủjìk?

Men kôrdìm ġašyḳ žardan uắdesìzdìk,
Ômìrdìṇ ḳyzyġynan kủder ủzdìk.
Žyly žủrek suydy, žara tủstì,
Šyḳpaġan šybyn žanmen kủn ôtkìzdìk.

Performed
by Ayaulym
Kamazhan

I HAD TO REVEAL ALL MY LOVE

VERSION I

I HAD TO REVEAL ALL MY LOVE

VERSION II

I HAD TO REVEAL ALL MY LOVE
VERSION III

I HAD TO REVEAL ALL MY LOVE
VERSION IV

I Had to Reveal All My Love

(Lyrics rendered from Alexander Pushkin, Tatyana's Letter to Onegin)

I had to reveal all my love
It could not be told in a word.
Sick at heart, I chose to approve
The injuries you conferred.

Defenceless and lost, I am now
A woman who knows dishonour.
Yet my heart must say what it knows,
So I dare to send this letter.

Abandoned, exposed, and alone,
I survive, while my love burns bright,
I could bear a life of disdain,
If each month, you came for a night.

When you're gone, I can't see your face,
Nor can I hear when you speak.
If I think of all I have lost
I know I won't sleep for a week.

Bridge translation by Assiya Issemberdiyeva

Tatânanyṇ Haty

Amal žoḳ – ḳajttìm bìldìrmej,
Âpyrmau, ḳajtìp ajtamyn.
Ḳojmajdy dertìṇ kùjdìrmej,
Ne salsaṇ da tartamyn.

Talajsyz, baḳsyz, men sorly,
Erìksìz attap ùâttan.
Ḳorlyḳḳa kôndìm bùl ḳùrly,
Bajḳalar halìm bùl hattan.

Ấlìmše men de ùâlyp,
'Bìldìremìn' dedìm, ôlsem de,
Šydar em kùjìp men žanyp,
Ajynda bìrer kôrsem de.

Bolmady kôrìp ḳaluġa
Estìp bìraz sôzìṇdì.
Šydar em bìr aj žatuġa
Ùzaḳ tùn žùmbaj kôzìmdì.

YOU WERE SENT TO ME BY GOD
VERSION I

YOU WERE SENT TO ME BY GOD
VERSION II

YOU WERE SENT TO ME BY GOD
VERSION III

YOU WERE SENT TO ME BY GOD
VERSION IV

YOU WERE SENT TO ME BY GOD
VERSION V

You Were Sent To Me By God
(Lyrics rendered from Alexander Pushkin, Tatyana's Second Letter to Onegin)

It was God's will that you found me,
Yet you spurned me as a bride.
I was a child, for all to see,
But my child's heart was denied.

Later I heard you left this place,
Disillusioned with the world.
How could you leave in such disgrace,
An innocent, loving child?

Was I not young, of tender years?
How could you not show pity?
I gave you all – my hopes, my fears –
You mocked my love with cruelty.

You came to me like a tiger,
Like a yearling, or a fawn,
I was ravaged by your anger,
I could barely struggle on.

I have no wish to speak of blame,
Yet I must say what I feel.
I am your friend, but fate's a game,
My heart was crushed in its wheels.

Bridge translation by Assiya Issemberdiyeva

YOU WERE SENT TO ME BY GOD

VERSION VI

Tatânanyṇ Sôzì

Ta̋ṇìrì ķosķan žar edìṇ sen,
Žar ete almaj ketìp eṇ.
Ol kezìmde bala edìm men,
Aâmasķa bekìp eṇ.

Talaķ etìp búl ġalamdy,
Boldy ma̋lìm ketkenìṇ,
Kìna̋sì žoķ žas adamdy
Ķatty soķķan ne etkenìṇ?

Elžìregen žas emes pe em?
Eppen ajtsaṇ žúbatyp.
Men ġašyķķa mas emes pe em?
Ketseṇ edì úzatyp.

Sen žaraly žolbarys eṇ,
Men kiìktìṇ laġy em.
Tìrì ķaldym, ôlmej a̋reṇ,
Ķatty batty tyrnaġyṇ.

Búl kìna̋ emes, a̋nšejìn naz,
Saġynamyn, ajtamyn.
Dosyṇ-aķpyn, taġdyr araz,
Tolġanamyn, ķajtemìn.

Performed
by Yerlan
Ryskali

FROM THE TEREK RIVER

From the Terek River

(lyrics after Lermontov)

O great Terek, river wild, thund'rous and strong,
Driving your path through cliff-sides and walls of stone,
White-capped with waves, like the mane of a crazed beast.
Ten-thousandfold, you ramble, flooding the plain.

Bubbling with joy, from your source, far in the hills.
You crossed the fields in uproar, you streamed through dales.
Kindly enough, so we thought, you laughed and played,
Yet down below, in the depths, your ways were wild.

You were a child of the high Caucasian way,
Nourished and bred, from the first, by mountain spray.
You set your course from Kazbek to the ocean,
Your destined home, and nothing can break your sway.

Breathless and lost, I have come, a kindred soul,
Far from the crowd: a lone man, through fields and hills
I come to you for refuge, like a brother.
I bring you gifts, accept them, with all goodwill.

Bridge translation by Assiya Issemberdiyeva

Terektìṇ Syjy

Asau Terek doldanyp, buyrḳanyp,
Taudy bu̇zyp žol salġan, tasty žaryp.
Arystannyṇ žalyndaj bu̇jra tolḳyn
Ajdaḥardaj bùktelìp, žùz tolġanyp.

Kavkazdan šyḳty žajnap, ḳylyp u-šu,
Tùzu žerden žol kernep u̇lġajdy su.
Ḳalyṇ ḳajrat bojynda, betì kùlìp,
Momynsynġan pìšìnmen aġady ḳu.

Kavkazdaj ḳu̇zda tuġan perzenttenmìn,
Bu̇lttyṇ sùtìn emìp eržetkenmìn.
Kazbekten, aġam, senì kôksep šyġyp,
Kìm ḳaḳtyḳsa žolymda kùjretkenmìn.

Aptyġyp asau ìnìṇ keldì, aḳsaḳal!
Tau, tasḳa, adamzatḳa salyp žanžal.
Dem alajyn dep keldìm, aš ḳojnyṇdy,
Sấlem-sauḳat ấkeldìm, ḳoš kôrìp al.

Performed by Askar Mukiyat

IN THE STILL OF NIGHT

VERSION I

IN THE STILL OF NIGHT

VERSION II

IN THE STILL OF NIGHT

VERSION III

In the Still of Night

In the still of night, the hills fall
Into an easy, restful sleep.
Night draws its blanket over all,
And silence descends on the steppe.

No clouds of dust on the trail,
No wind blows in through the dell.
And peace will come, without fail,
Take courage, friend, all is well.

Bridge translation by Assiya Issemberdiyeva

Ķaraņġy Tùnde Tau Ķalġyp

Ķaraņġy tùnde tau ķalġyp,
Ùjķyġa keter balbyrap.
Dalany žym-žyrt, del-sal ķyp,
Tùn basady salbyrap.

Šaņ šyġarmas žol daġy,
Sìlkìne almas žapyraķ.
Tynšyġarsyņ sen daġy,
Sabyr ķylsaņ azyraķ.

Performed
by Kairat
Baibosynov

ŽOĶTAU*

Žoķtau*

(Written by Abai to Mağyš, Ãbdìrahman's Wife)*

Lord, you must know, in this life
I have borne so much through the years,
When my mother died, I was crushed,
At five I wept bitter tears.

The one who is locked in their grief,
They can't hide the pain, or the tears.
For a lifetime, I've missed my love:
Grief made things worse, through the years.

It was you who foiled every wish,
You were the source of my cares,
Because of you, my hopes were dashed.
Ấbìš was gone; I despaired.

My husband Ấbìš, gone to dust.
The best of his kind, the flower.
Into the earth you sent him.
And though I should have been there

I was absent – I, his wife!
At twenty two, a mourner,
Widow-woman, dowager.
All down the years I have never

Known comfort or peace in this life.
Your will has cut me like a knife.
He who was my love, my life:
Now gone from my sight, forever.

Bridge translation by Aknur Toleubayeva

**Žoķtau* – a memorial song, also a genre of Kazakh folk poetry, usually composed and performed by the closest female relatives of a deceased.

* Ấbdìrahman (Ấbìš) Ôṣkenbaev (1869–95) – Abai's son from his first wife Dìldấ. Abai was very close to Ấbdìrahman, who was educated in Semej, Tyumen and Saint Petersburg. After falling ill, Ấbdìrahman passed away in 1895 in the city of Almaty.

Ấbdìrahmannyn̦ Ấjelì Maġyšk̦a Abai Šyġaryp Bergen Žok̦tau

Ajnalajyn K̦ùdaj-au,
K̦apalyk̦ saldyn̦ žasymnan.
Šešenin̦ zaryn tarttyrdyn̦
Bes žasymda basymnan.

Sôjlemej bende šydamas
K̦ajġy otyna ašynġan.
Žarymdy kôrmej neše žyl,
K̦apalyk̦ty asyrġan.

Žarymdy alyp k̦or k̦yldyn̦
Žas ômìrde tasynġan.
Ajyryp, ot k̦yp ôrtedìn̦,
Ấbìš syndy asyldan.

Ấbìštì alyp kùl k̦yldyn̦,
K̦yzyldy gùldì žasyldan.
Tym bolmasa k̦yzmet k̦yp,
Ôtkìzbedìm k̦asymnan.

Žiyrma ekì žasymda
Men ajryldym žarymnan.
Žaryk̦, sấule kôrmedìm
Šyk̦k̦aly ana k̦arnynan.

... Ôzgeše bolyp žaralġan,
Ajyryldym k̦alk̦am žarymnan.
Sol k̦alk̦amdy k̦ojmaġan
Zamana netken tar edì?

TORŽORĠA

Performed
by Rustem
Nurkenov

MAY NIGHT (MAJ TÙNÌ)

Performed by Rustem Nurkenov

ŽELDÌRME

NOTES

'Octaves' ('Segìz aâķ', Version I) transcribed in 1920 in Akmola region by Alvin Bimboes (1878–1942) from a singer and poet Mùstafa Nùrbaev's performance. First published in *Abaidyņ muzykalyķ tvorčestvosy* (N7), ed. by Boris Yerzakovich, Almaty, 1954.

'Octaves' ('Segìz aâķ', Version II) transcribed in 1922 in Orenburg by Alexander Zatayevich (1869–1936) from Ķùstaj Myrzabekov and Kắrìm Ķašķymbaev's performance. First published in *A.Zatayevich. Ắr žyldar ắnderì* (N20), compiled by Varvara Dernova, Almaty, 1971.

'Octaves' ('Segìz aâķ', Version III) transcribed in 1934 in Almaty by Alexander Zatayevich (1869–1936) from a poet Temìrbolat Arġynbaev's (1887–1940) performance. First published in *Abaidyņ muzykalyķ tvorčestvosy* (N5), ed. by Boris Yerzakovich, Almaty, 1954.

'Octaves' ('Segìz aâķ', Version IV) transcribed in Semej in 1935 by Latif Hamidi (1906–83) from Abai's kinsman Ắrham Ysķaķov's (1885–1962) performance. First published in *Abaidyņ muzykalyķ tvorčestvosy* (N3), ed. by Boris Yerzakovich, Almaty, 1954.

'Octaves' ('Segìz aâķ', Version V) transcribed in 1939 in Almaty by Latif Hamidi (1906–83) from a singer Ķuan Lekerov's (1896–1955) performance. First published in *Abaidyņ muzykalyķ tvorčestvosy* (N4), ed. by Boris Yerzakovich, Almaty, 1954.

'Octaves' ('Segìz aâķ', Version VI) transcribed in Almaty by Latif Hamidi (1906–83) from a singer Žùsìpbek Elebekov's (1904–77) performance. First published in *Abaidyņ muzykalyķ tvorčestvosy* (N6), ed. by Boris Yerzakovich, Almaty, 1954.

'Octaves' ('Segìz aâķ', Version VII) transcribed in Almaty in 1954 from a singer Ķali Bajžanov's (1877–1966) performance; notated in 1984 by Ķajrolla Žùzbasov (b.1941). First published in *Abaidyņ ắnderì men kùjlerì* compiled by Nùrġali Nùsìpžanov (b. 1937) and Anar Erkebaj (b.1978), Almaty, 2012.

'Octaves' ('Segìz aâķ', Version VIII) recorded on a tape in Almaty from a performance by Abai's granddaughter Mắken Mùhametžanova (b. 1912); notated in 1984 by Ķajrolla Žùzbasov (b.1941). First published in *Abaidyņ ắnderì men kùjlerì* compiled by Nùrġali Nùsìpžanov (b. 1937) and Anar Erkebaj (b.1978), Almaty, 2012.

'I have grown weary' ('Ķor boldy žanym', Version I) transcribed in Orenburg by Alexander Zatayevich (1869–1936) Eskendìr Dajrabaev's performance. First published in *Abaidyņ muzykalyķ tvorčestvosy* (N10), ed. by Boris Yerzakovich, Almaty, 1954.

'I have grown weary' ('Ķor boldy žanym', Version II) transcribed in 1934 in Almaty by Yevgeny Brusilovsky (1905–81) from the great singer Ắmìre Ķašaubaev's (1888–1934) performance. First published in *Abaidyņ muzykalyķ tvorčestvosy* (N9), ed. by Boris Yerzakovich, Almaty, 1954.

'I have grown weary' ('Ķor boldy žanym', Version III) transcribed in Semej in 1935 by Latif Hamidi (1905–81) from Abai's kinsman Ắrham Ysķaķov's (1885–1962) performance. First published in *Abaidyņ muzykalyķ tvorčestvosy* (N8), ed. by Boris Yerzakovich, Almaty, 1954.

'I have grown weary' ('Ķor boldy žanym', Version IV) recorded on a tape in Almaty from a performance by Abai's granddaughter Mắken Mùhametžanova (b. 1912); notated in 1984 by Ķajrolla Žùzbasov (b.1941). First published in *Abaidyņ ắnderì men kùjlerì* compiled by Nùrġali Nùsìpžanov (b. 1937) and Anar Erkebaj (b.1978), Almaty, 2012.

'What do you want from me?' ('Sen menì ne etesìņ?', Version I) transcribed in Semej in 1935 by Latif Hamidi (1906–83) from Abai's kinsman Ắrham Ysķaķov's (1885–1962) performance. First published in *Abaidyņ muzykalyķ tvorčestvosy* (N8), ed. by Boris Yerzakovich, Almaty, 1954.

'What do you want from me?' ('Sen menì ne etesìņ?', Version II) recorded on a tape in Almaty from a performance by Abai's granddaughter Mắken Mùhametžanova (b. 1912); notated in 1984 by Ķajrolla Žùzbasov (b.1941). First published in *Abaidyņ ắnderì men kùjlerì* compiled by Nùrġali Nùsìpžanov (b. 1937) and Anar Erkebaj (b.1978), Almaty, 2012.

'Blessings on you' ('Ajttym sắlem ķalam ķas', Version I) transcribed by Boris Yerzakovich (1908–97) from a poet Temìrbolat Arġynbaev's (1887–1940) performance. First published in *Abaidyņ muzykalyķ tvorčestvosy* (N12), ed. by Boris Yerzakovich, Almaty, 1954.

'Blessings on you' ('Ajttym sắlem ķalam ķas', Version II) transcribed in Semej in 1935 by Latif Hamidi (1905–81) from a performance by Abai's kinsman Ắrham Ysķaķov (1885–1962). First published in *Abaidyņ muzykalyķ tvorčestvosy* (N13), ed. by Boris Yerzakovich, Almaty, 1954.

'The child who is loved' ('Ata-anaġa kôz ķuanyš') transcribed in 1939 in Almaty by Latif Hamidi (1906–83) from a singer Ķuan Lekerov's (1896–1955) performance. First published in *Abaidyņ muzykalyķ tvorčestvosy* (N21), ed. by Boris Yerzakovich, Almaty, 1954.

'My soul, you are charmed by nothing' ('Ôzgege, kôņìlìm toârsyņ', Version I) transcribed in 1922 in Orenburg by Alexander Zatayevich (1869–1936) from Müsylmanķül Ắbsalyķov's performance. First published in *Abaidyņ muzykalyķ tvorčestvosy* (N19), ed. by Boris Yerzakovich, Almaty, 1954.

'My soul, you are charmed by nothing' ('Ôzgege, kôņìlìm toârsyņ', Version II) recorded on a tape in Almaty from a performance by Abai's granddaughter Mǟken Mühametžanova (b. 1912); notated in 1984 by Ķajrolla Žùzbasov (b.1941). First published in *Abaidyņ ǟnderì men kùjlerì* compiled by Nürġali Nùsìpžanov (b. 1937) and Anar Erkebaj (b.1978), Almaty, 2012.

'The Apple of My Eye' ('Kôzìmnìņ ķarasy', Version I) transcribed in Semej in 1935 by Latif Hamidi (1906–83) from Abai's kinsman Ǟrham Ysķaķov's (1885–1962) performance. First published in *Abaidyņ muzykalyķ tvorčestvosy* (N22), ed. by Boris Yerzakovich, Almaty, 1954.

'The Apple of My Eye' ('Kôzìmnìņ ķarasy', Version I) transcribed in Almaty in 1939 by Boris Yerzakovich (1906–83) from a singer Žùsìpbek Elebekov's (1904–77) performance. First published in *Abaidyņ muzykalyķ tvorčestvosy* (N6), ed. by Boris Yerzakovich, Almaty, 1954.

'The Apple of My Eye' ('Kôzìmnìņ ķarasy', Version III) transcribed in Orenburg in 1922 by Alexander Zatayevich (1869–1936) from Serġazy Tamteev's performance. First published in *A.Zatayevich. Ǟr žyldar ǟnderì* (N120), compiled by Varvara Dernova, Almaty, 1971.

'The Apple of My Eye' ('Kôzìmnìņ ķarasy', Version IV) recorded on a tape recorder in Almaty from a performance by Abai's granddaughter Mǟken Mühametžanova (b. 1912); notated in 1984 by Ķajrolla Žùzbasov (b.1941). First published in *Abaidyņ ǟnderì men kùjlerì* compiled by Nürġali Nùsìpžanov (b. 1937) and Anar Erkebaj (b.1978), Almaty, 2012.

'Hypocrite' ('Bojy bùlġaņ', Version I) transcribed in Semej in 1935 by Latif Hamidi (1906–83) from Abai's kinsman Ǟrham Ysķaķov's (1885–1962) performance. First published in *Abaidyņ muzykalyķ tvorčestvosy* (N24), ed. by Boris Yerzakovich, Almaty, 1954.

'Hypocrite' ('Bojy bùlġaņ', Version II) transcribed in Almaty in 1939 by Boris Yerzakovich (1906–83) from a singer Žùsìpbek Elebekov's (1904–77) performance. First published in *Abaidyņ muzykalyķ tvorčestvosy* (N25), ed. by Boris Yerzakovich, Almaty, 1954.

'Hypocrite' ('Bojy bùlġaņ', Version III) recorded on a tape recorder in Almaty from a performance by Abai's granddaughter Mǟken Mühametžanova (b. 1912); notated in 1984 by Ķajrolla Žùzbasov (b.1941). First published in *Abaidyņ ǟnderì men kùjlerì* compiled by Nürġali Nùsìpžanov (b. 1937) and Anar Erkebaj (b.1978), Almaty, 2012.

'The earth turns slow in autumn' ('Ķarašada ômìr tùr', Version I) transcribed in Almaty by Latif Hamidi (1906–83) from a singer Žùsìpbek Elebekov's (1904–77) performance. First published in *Abaidyņ muzykalyķ tvorčestvosy* (N29), ed. by Boris Yerzakovich, Almaty, 1954.

'The earth turns slow in autumn' ('Ķarašada ômìr tùr', Version II) recorded on a tape recorder in Almaty from a performance by Abai's granddaughter Mắken Mùhametžanova (b. 1912); notated in 1984 by Ķajrolla Žùzbasov (b.1941). First published in *Abaidyņ ănderì men kùjlerì* compiled by Nùrġali Nùsìpžanov (b. 1937) and Anar Erkebaj (b.1978), Almaty, 2012.

'The Moon' ('Želsìz tùnde žaryķ aj', Version I) transcribed in Semej in 1935 by Latif Hamidi (1906–83) from Abai's kinsman Ắrham Ysķaķov's (1885–1962) performance. First published in *Abaidyņ muzykalyķ tvorčestvosy* (N32), ed. by Boris Yerzakovich, Almaty, 1954.

'The Moon' ('Želsìz tùnde žaryķ aj', Version II) transcribed in 1939 in Almaty by Latif Hamidi (1906–83) from a singer Ķuan Lekerov's (1896–1955) performance. First published in *Abaidyņ muzykalyķ tvorčestvosy* (N31), ed. by Boris Yerzakovich, Almaty, 1954

'You could not love me, nor I, you' ('Sùjsìne almadym, sùjmedìm') transcribed in 1954 in Almaty by Boris Yerzakovich (1908–97) from the famous writer Mùhtar Ắuezov's (1897–1961) performance. First published in *Abaidyņ muzykalyķ tvorčestvosy* (N36), ed. by Boris Yerzakovich, Almaty, 1954

'If one outweighs another' ('Bìreuden bìreu artylsa,' Version I) transcribed in 1934 in Almaty by Yevgeny Brusilovsky (1905–81) from the great singer Ắmìre Ķašaubaev's (1888–1934) performance. First published in *Abaidyņ muzykalyķ tvorčestvosy* (N2), ed. by Boris Yerzakovich, Almaty, 1954.

'If one outweighs another' ('Bìreuden bìreu artylsa,' Version II) transcribed in Semej in 1935 by Latif Hamidi (1905–81) from Abai's kinsman Ắrham Ysķaķov's (1885–1962) performance. First published in *Abaidyņ muzykalyķ tvorčestvosy* (N2), ed. by Boris Yerzakovich, Almaty, 1954.

'If one outweighs another' ('Bìreuden bìreu artylsa', Version III) recorded on a tape recorder in Almaty from a performance by Abai's granddaughter Mắken Mùhametžanova (b. 1912); notated in 1984 by Ķajrolla Žùzbasov (b.1941). First published in *Abaidyņ ănderì men kùjlerì* compiled by Nùrġali Nùsìpžanov (b. 1937) and Anar Erkebaj (b.1978), Almaty, 2012.

'The mood is strong' ('Kôņìl ķùsy ķùjķylžyr šartarapķa') transcribed in Semej in 1935 by Latif Hamidi (1906–83) from Abai's kinsman Ắrham Ysķaķov's (1885–1962) performance. First published in *Abaidyņ muzykalyķ tvorčestvosy* (N30), ed. by Boris Yerzakovich, Almaty, 1954.

Remembering Youth ('Esìņde bar ma žas kùnìņ') recorded on a tape recorder in Almaty from a performance by Abai's granddaughter Mắken Mùhametžanova (b. 1912); notated in 1984 by Ķajrolla Žùzbasov (b.1941). First published in *Abaidyņ ănderì men kùjlerì* compiled by Nùrġali Nùsìpžanov (b. 1937) and Anar Erkebaj (b.1978), Almaty, 2012.

'If I should die' (Ôlsem, ornym ķara žer syz bolmaj ma?) transcribed in Semej in 1935 by Latif Hamidi (1906–83) from Abai's kinsman Ắrham Ysķaķov's (1885–1962) performance. First published in *Abaidyņ muzykalyķ tvorčestvosy* (N33), ed. by Boris Yerzakovich, Almaty, 1954.

'Fine outside, I'm dead within' ('Ìšìm ôlgen, syrtym sau') transcribed in Semej in 1935 by Latif Hamidi (1906–83) from Abai's kinsman Ắrham Ysķaķov's (1885–1962) performance. First published in *Abaidyņ muzykalyķ tvorčestvosy* (N19), ed. by Boris Yerzakovich, Almaty, 1954.

'The grey mist turns' ('Sùrġylt tùman dym bùrkìp', Version I) transcribed in Semej in 1935 by Latif Hamidi (1906–83) from Abai's kinsman Ắrham Ysķaķov's (1885–1962) performance. First published in *Abaidyņ muzykalyķ tvorčestvosy* (N26), ed. by Boris Yerzakovich, Almaty, 1954.

'The grey mist turns' ('Sùrġylt tùman dym bùrkìp', Version II) transcribed in Almaty in 1953 by Boris Yerzakovich (1908–97) from a poet Sadyķ Ķasimanov's (1902–77) performance. First published in *Abaidyņ muzykalyķ tvorčestvosy* (N27), ed. by Boris Yerzakovich, Almaty, 1954.

'The grey mist turns' ('Sùrġylt tùman dym bùrkìp', Version III) recorded on a tape recorder in Almaty from a performance by Abai's granddaughter Mắken Mùhametžanova (b. 1912); notated in 1984 by Ķajrolla Žùzbasov (b.1941). First published in *Abaidyņ ănderì men kùjlerì* compiled by Nùrġali Nùsìpžanov (b. 1937) and Anar Erkebaj (b.1978), Almaty, 2012.

'A tree fell' ('Men kôrdìm ùzyn ķajyņ ķùlaġanyn', Version I) transcribed in 1939 in Almaty by Latif Hamidi (1906–83) from the famous writer Mùhtar Ắuezov's (1897–1961) performance. First published in *Abaidyņ muzykalyķ tvorčestvosy* (N34), ed. by Boris Yerzakovich, Almaty, 1954.

A tree fell' ('Men kôrdìm ùzyn ķajyņ ķùlaġanyn', Version II) transcribed in 1939 by Boris Yerzakovich (1908–97) from a poet Temìrbolat Arġynbaev's (1887–1940) performance. First published in *Abaidyņ ănderì men kùjlerì* compiled by Nùrġali Nùsìpžanov (b. 1937) and Anar Erkebaj (b.1978), Almaty, 2012.

A tree fell' ('Men kôrdim ùzyn ķajyņ ķùlaġanyn', Version III) recorded on a tape recorder in Almaty from a performance by Abai's granddaughter Mắken Mùhametžanova (b. 1912); notated in 1984 by Ķajrolla Žùzbasov (b.1941). First published in *Abaidyņ ănderì men kùjlerì* compiled by Nùrġali Nùsìpžanov (b. 1937) and Anar Erkebaj (b.1978), Almaty, 2012.

'I had to reveal all my love' ('Tatânanyņ haty', Version I) transcribed in 1922 in Orenburg by Alexander Zatayevich (1869–1936) from Šắrìp Medetov's (b. 1909) performance. First published in *A.Zatayevich. Ắr žyldar ănderì* (N39), compiled by Varvara Dernova, Almaty, 1971.

'I had to reveal all my love' ('Tatânanyṇ haty', Version II) transcribed in 1922 in Orenburg by Alexander Zatayevich (1869–1936) from Balķiâ Ìsķûlova and Zura Bajzaķova's performance. First published in *A.Zatayevich. Ãr žyldar ãnderì* (N39), compiled by Varvara Dernova, Almaty, 1971.

'I had to reveal all my love' ('Tatânanyṇ haty', Version III) transcribed in Semej in 1935 by Latif Hamidi (1905–81) from Abai's kinsman Ãrham Ysķaķov's (1885–1962) performance. First published in *Abaidyṇ muzykalyķ tvorčestvosy* (N4), ed. by Boris Yerzakovich, Almaty, 1954.

'I had to reveal all my love' ('Tatânanyṇ haty', Version IV) recorded on a tape recorder in Almaty from a performance by Abai's granddaughter Mãken Mûhametžanova (b. 1912); notated in 1984 by Ķajrolla Žùzbasov (b.1941). First published in *Abaidyṇ ãnderì men kùjlerì* compiled by Nûrġali Nùsìpžanov (b. 1937) and Anar Erkebaj (b.1978), Almaty, 2012.

'You were sent to me by God' ('Tatânanyṇ sôzì', Version I) transcribed in 1920 in Aķmola region by Alvin Bimboes (1878–1942) from Nazifa Ķûlžanova's (1887–1933) performance. First published in *Narodnaya muzyka v Kazakhstane* without lyrics (N7), compiled by Varvara Dernova, Almaty, 1967.

'You were sent to me by God' ('Tatânanyṇ sôzì', Version II) transcribed in 1922 in Orenburg by Alexander Zatayevich (1869–1936). First published without lyrics in *100 pesen* by Alexander Zatayevich (N120), edited by Ahmet Žûbanov et al, Moscow, 1963.

'You were sent to me by God' ('Tatânanyṇ sôzì', Version III) transcribed in 1922 in Orenburg by Alexander Zatayevich (1869–1936) from Osman Ķašaġûlov's performance. First published without lyrics in *100 pesen* by Alexander Zatayevich (N129), edited by Ahmet Žûbanov et al, Moscow, 1963.

'You were sent to me by God' ('Tatânanyṇ sôzì', Version IV) transcribed in 1930 in Moscow by Alexander Zatayevich (1869–1936) from a writer Sãbit Mûķanov's (1900–73) performance. First published without lyrics in *A.Zatayevich. Ãr žyldar ãnderì* (N120), compiled by Varvara Dernova, Almaty, 1971.

'You were sent to me by God' ('Tatânanyṇ sôzì', Version V) transcribed in Semej in 1935 by Latif Hamidi (1906–83) from Abai's kinsman Ãrham Ysķaķov's (1885–1962) performance. First published in *Abaidyṇ muzykalyķ tvorčestvosy* (N17), ed. by Boris Yerzakovich, Almaty, 1954.

'From the Terek River' ('Terektìṇ Syjy') recorded on a tape recorder in Almaty from a performance by Abai's granddaughter Mãken Mûhametžanova (b. 1912); notated in 1984 by Ķajrolla Žùzbasov (b.1941). First published in *Abaidyṇ ãnderì men kùjlerì* compiled by Nûrġali Nùsìpžanov (b. 1937) and

Anar Erkebaj (b.1978), Almaty, 2012.
'In the still of night' ('Ķaraņġy tùnde tau ķalġyp', Version I) transcribed in Almaty in 1944 by Latif Hamidi (1906–83) from a singer Žùsìpbek Elebekov's (1904–77) performance. First published in *Abaidyņ muzykalyķ tvorčestvosy* (N28), ed. by Boris Yerzakovich, Almaty, 1954.

'In the still of night' ('Ķaraņġy tùnde tau ķalġyp', Version II) transcribed by Ķajrolla Žùzbasov (b.1941) from a singer Ķali Bajžanov's (1877–1966) performance. First published in *Abaidyņ muzykalyķ tvorčestvosy* (N28), ed. by Boris Yerzakovich, Almaty, 1954.

'In the still of night' ('Ķaraņġy tùnde tau ķalġyp', Version III) recorded on a tape recorder in Almaty from a performance by Abai's granddaughter Mắken Mùhametžanova (b. 1912); notated in 1984 by Ķajrolla Žùzbasov (b.1941). First published in *Abaidyņ ǟnderì men kùjlerì* compiled by Nùrġali Nùsìpžanov (b. 1937) and Anar Erkebaj (b.1978), Almaty, 2012.

Žoķtau (Written by Abai to Maġyš, Ǟbdìrahman's Wife) recorded on a tape recorder in Almaty from a performance by Abai's granddaughter Mắken Mùhametžanova (b. 1912); notated in 1984 by Ķajrolla Žùzbasov (b.1941). First published in *Abaidyņ ǟnderì men kùjlerì* compiled by Nùrġali Nùsìpžanov (b. 1937) and Anar Erkebaj (b.1978), Almaty, 2012.

'Toržorġa' transcribed in 1983 by Uǟli Bekenov (b. 1934) from Ġajsa Sarmurzin's (1904–87) performance. First published in *Abaidyņ ǟnderì men kùjlerì* compiled by Nùrġali Nùsìpžanov (b. 1937) and Anar Erkebaj (b.1978), Almaty, 2012.

'May Night' ('Maj tùnì') recorded in 1983 by Uǟli Bekenov (b. 1934) from Ġajsa Sarmurzin's (1904–87) performance. First published in *Abaidyņ ǟnderì men kùjlerì* compiled by Nùrġali Nùsìpžanov (b. 1937) and Anar Erkebaj (b.1978), Almaty, 2012.

'*Želdìrme*' (also referred to as '**Abaidyņ Želdìrmesì**') recorded in Ķatonķaraġaj *auyl* (village) of Eastern Kazakhstan region by Ķajrolla Žùzbasov (b. 1941) from Hamza Demšinov's performance. First published in *Abaidyņ ǟnderì men kùjlerì* compiled by Nùrġali Nùsìpžanov (b. 1937) and Anar Erkebaj (b.1978), Almaty, 2012.

Note on transcription. The International ISO 9 Standard of Romanising the Cyrillic Characters has been applied while transliterating the Kazakh terms, including geographical and personal names, except for the author's name, which appears as the 'Abai' widely used in English-language resources.

Printed in Dunstable, United Kingdom

78876614R10048